THE HILLEL LITTLE BOOKS

will deal with issues of fundamental importance to Jewish college students. Since they seek to stimulate discussion and study, they will make demands upon their readers. In that specific sense, they will not be "popular" volumes. Written by men of many, variant points of view, they are not intended as final answers but as a challenge to further reading — in the spirit of Hillel the sage, himself:

".....a certain pagan came before Shammai and said to him, 'Convert me — but on condition that you teach me the entire Torah while I stand on one foot!' But Shammai drove him away with the builder's cubit that was in his hand. Then he came before Hillel who said, 'What is hateful to you, do not do to your neighbor — This is the entire Torah. The rest is the commentary thereon. . . . .

GO, STUDY!"

SHABBAT 31 A

What Is
This Jewish
Heritage?

HILLEL LITTLE BOOKS

What Is This Jewish Heritage?

by Ludwig Lewisohn

B'NAI B'RITH HILLEL FOUNDATIONS

NEW YORK   1954

CONTENTS

What Is

This Jewish

Heritage?

WHAT IS A JEW

What is a Jew? What is it to *be* a Jew? Are Jews
a religious community, like the Roman or Greek
Churches? Or are Jews an ethnic group, like the
Negroes? Or are they a secular community, formed
by historic forces, which is a vague enough term,
like the Danes or the Dutch?

A little accurate thinking will show that each one
of these analogies breaks down hopelessly as soon
as it is pressed.

No merely religious community ever had a specific homeland nor an authentic language created by
itself as the expression of its unique character nor,
above all, thousands of passionate adherents who
are indifferent to religion or even hostile to it.

An ethnic group, on the other hand, has or is
supposed to have definite physical characteristics,
such as skin pigmentation or hair texture or eye-
shape. Trivial as even these marks are, Jews do not
possess them. Even the so-called Jewish nose is at
least as prevalent among "Indo-European" Arme-
nians as it is among "Semitic" Jews. So it is clear
that Jews are neither a *merely* religious body nor an
ethnic group.

Our trouble becomes even acuter when we seek
to define Jews as a mere national community, shaped
by historic forces, like the Danes or the Dutch.
Danes and Netherlanders, relatively late converts
to Christianity, leaders in the Protestant revolt, have
no autochthonous religion — none, that means,

which they themselves originated. Jews have. When these Nordic peoples leave their own lands, they merge easily with the peoples and the cultures of their new environment. What are the Dutch of New Amsterdam but a shadow and a pleasant legend to-day? In what specific sense was Franklin Delano Roosevelt a Dutchman? But though the Jews were driven from their recently recovered homeland eighteen-hundred years ago, a distinguished American public servant, like Mr. Mordecai Joseph Ezekiel, whose family has been on these shores nearly as long as the Roosevelts, is by name and fame, by spiritual configuration and outer destiny, a Jew.

In view of these facts, too simple and obvious to be denied, it is not surprising that responsible thinkers have described and defined the Jewish people not only as a unique group, but as one torn out of the general context of history. Modern historians are fond of attributing a pattern to the existence of peoples. Each people and its culture arises, flourishes, declines and disappears from the scene of history. The Jewish people made its historic appearance, as we shall see, in quite a normal fashion. Yet the pattern of its history is violently abnormal. It never flourished greatly in terms of power. It knew defeat and desperate catastrophe over and over again. Yet from each historic grave it re-arose; it survived; it lived to re-affirm its changeless character and historic function.

What was the source within history of that power

of survival and renewal which has taken place from age to age down to that birth of the State of Israel from the ashes of the six-million martyrs, an event within the memory of the youngest Jew now living and seeking to interpret his destiny and its meaning? So far as human insight extends, the source of that perpetual life and perpetual power of re-birth must be, cannot but be, in that transcendent experience at the foot of Sinai which welded a group of rude clans and fugitives from oppression into a people whose fundamental character was stamped and moulded then.

Petulant men with minds frozen thirty years ago will call this explanation "mystical" in the illiterate usage of that word as anything beyond the grasp of the most mechanical and empty understanding. Mature and unbiased reflection will show that this explanation and this alone, precisely this, like any respectable hypothesis in the sciences, serves to account for the historic phenomena which no one denies. This hypothesis alone *works*. It alone explains the character, the history, the ever recurrent fate of the Jewish people.

WHO IS A JEW

It is clear, then, that the question: what is a Jew, is an intricate one. Though it may seem a purely theoretical question, the answer given to it has very concrete consequences in the conduct of life. But in America today there are even more searching and immediate questions, questions that involve what William James used to call living options or choices. And these questions are: *Who is a Jew?* And: *What does it mean to be a Jew?*

People with lazy minds use verbal rubber-stamps to keep the facts of life at a distance. And one of these verbal rubber-stamps by which they seek to evade reality is "the accident of birth." Now the word "accident" is in itself invariably an evasion or a confession of ignorance. We call "accident" any fact or event for which we cannot account. Those who use the word do not ever pretend to give up the notion of cause and effect. They know that a universe without the category of causality would fall to pieces. Without the chain of cause and effect there would be no science, there would be no observational knowledge nor the laws, those statements of recurrence, which science derives from such knowledge. In other words: there are no "accidents". There are only facts and events, of which the causes are unknown to us.

Birth, however, has been called an "accident" out of quite impure motives. There is no event — no result or issue — of which the causes are more clearly known. If you are known as a Jew and if you acknowledge yourself to be one, it is so because a chain of cause and effect arising in an immemorial antiquity has not been broken. If you are known as a Jew and know yourself to be a Jew, you have two Jewish parents and four Jewish grand-parents and eight Jewish great-grandparents and sixteen Jewish great-great-grandparents. Around the year 1700 you had 512 Jewish ancestors and around the year 1670 you had 1024. Pursue this chain of arithmetical progression. No aspect of human destiny can be more deeply rooted in either nature or history than the destiny of birth.

Let us repeat these words: one's birth is destined by both nature and history. Yet the universe is not one of inescapable determinism. At any point the ancestral chain could have been broken. It could have been broken by apostasy or by intermarriage or by both. But had the chain been broken in your case, had a single one of your direct ancestors abandoned the community of Israel, you would no more be a Jew nor would you be known as a Jew nor know yourself to be one. The slightest observation of the contemporary scene, as well as of historic scenes, confirms this. Apostasy or intermarriage without the conversion of the Gentile spouse still leaves him who practices either a recognizable Jew. But the character of his children is already blurred and his grandchildren are no more known as Jews nor know themselves as such.

Now from this circumstance there arises a fact, a truth, of the very highest moral import. All of that great group of men and women, of fathers and mothers, who begot and bore you — all *willed* to be Jews; all affirmed their humanity within and through their Jewishness and clung to their Judaism in good and evil days. Blank escape from medieval

Ghetto and later community was always possible and was practiced from time to time. Until the appearance of Hitler all the prizes of the world were in many lands open to the apostate. Not one of that great and venerable company of *your* fathers and mothers dreamed of avoidance and escape.

Hence, if today you are known as a Jew and know yourself to be one, you are what you are not only within the order of nature and biological descent, but within the order of moral freedom, of willing and of choice, of loyalty to a historic reality and to a set of inherent values of transcendent worth.

You, then, who are a Jew, face an objective vital fact, an inescapable existential fact, of quite incalculable gravity and significance.

THE CHOICE

The next and, of course, the decisive question is: What will you *do* with that fact, the objective fact of your Jewishness?

You can try mere avoidance, mere negation of the implications of being what you are, the feeble mimicry of undifferentiated Americanism. But this feeble mimicry will always remain a futile gesture. You will be living behind a mask, at the mercy of a word, an implication, an exclusion, whether intentional or not, whether dictated by a resistance to your Jewishness or not, from any choice, group, fellowship, club, neighborhood, organization. Your life will be precarious and equivocal. Your social contacts will be restricted within the narrowest limits and your moral dynamism reduced to a minimum. Far from being free, you will be the most unfree of mortals. For the only freedom that man has is the freedom of his moral choice, the freedom to choose the law which he shall obey. And that freedom can be exercised only within the realm or area of one's own vital reality. Our fathers called this freedom identification of their will with God's will; a contemporary psychiatrist calls it "voluntary affirmation of the obligatory"; a modern philosopher bids us to incorporate our necessities into our willing.

This quite ultimate insight of human wisdom is universal. It is shared by the avowed pagans of the world. Nietzsche cries: *Werde der du bist*! "Become what you *are*!" In other words: seek your destined being; recover your true reality. That true reality is often hidden from us by illusions, false adaptations, social pressures. These illusions are to be swept aside, these false adaptations to be held unworthy, these social pressures to be resisted. The true self is to be sought. And that true self living in a community of true selves — such is the ideal of a harmonious and well-adjusted life.

What is so often and with such feeble facility called adjustment among us in America today is the adaptation of a personality which has not found itself to social patterns wholly irrelevant to that true self.

Another magnificent and unexpected summing up

of this matter of freedom and obedience and the true self of man is found in D. H. Lawrence's "Studies in Classic American Literature":

"Men are free when they are obeying some deep inward voice of religious belief. Obeying from within. Men are free when they belong to a living, organic, *believing* community, active in fulfilling some unfulfilled, perhaps unrealized purpose. Not when they are escaping to some wild west. The most unfree souls go west, and shout of freedom. The shout is a rattling of chains, always was."

How pertinent that is to the total Jewish situation! But Lawrence, something of a conventional anti-Semite in his own person, derived this cleaving, universal insight from his own agonized experience of the modern substitution of whim and self-will (where there is no true self) for rational freedom. The latest and also the profoundest observation on this matter, an observation that clears the air and lifts the heart, has been made by Thomas Mann:

"What is freedom? Only the indifferent (the undifferentiated) is 'free'. Whatever is characteristic is never 'free'; it is stamped, determined, bound."

Thomas Mann, needless to say, was not thinking of Jews when he wrote these words. He was thinking of the universal mysteries of choice and law and form; he was wondering whether a certain kind of lawless freedom was not of necessity issuing in sterility today in both art and life. He was seeking a principle that is at the core of both society and nature. Form is freedom; formlessness is slavery; conformity to one's destined form is the highest exercise of man's moral freedom. Mann meant the same thing that Franz Kafka meant when he said: "Sin is recoiling from one's own mission."

For Jews, finally, the whole matter has been summed up by that heroic sage of our day, Dr. Leo Baeck:

> "What necessity requires is willed; the realization of one's difference is transformed into a resolution to be different."

We come back to the unescapable, objective fact of your Jewishness. What is to be done with it? According to all wisdom and experience, it is evidently the guide to that true and deep self which is the real you, the ultimate existential reality of your life and being. That real being, that true self is to be sought; it is to be recovered in so far as it has been blurred or lost; it is to be affirmed by personal acts and by commitment to the eternal community of Israel; it is to be deepened and heightened by love, by knowledge, by aspiration. It is to become the principle of integration of the whole man, of that human being who can be *whole* (entire), — which is the same word as *hale* (healthy) — only by being in the fullest sense what evidently (by the law of nature or of God) it was meant to be.

FREEDOM TO CHOOSE

Why all these words? Why this fairly elaborate train of reasoning? One is born a Jew, one lives as a Jew, one dies a Jew. Isn't it, as a matter of clear common sense more profitable, more intelligent, even more fun (or less painful) to be an instructed Jew, a free Jew, a happy Jew? Why is this massive and yet simple matter debated in slightly whining essays, in more than slightly confused debates?

The answer to these questions must be brief and sharp: the spirit of liberty is on the wane. It has been on the wane throughout the Western world for several decades. It is on the wane among us in America today. The "crowd culture", so trenchantly stigmatised by an eminent Christian educator, Cannon Bernard Iddings Bell of Chicago, is engulfing us all.

A distinguished refugee from Germany, an affirmative Jew who, as such, had been a German statesman both under the Wilhelmian Empire and the Weimar Republic, used with a tragic conviction to declare that none of his German colleagues and former friends had been taken in by the foul lies and brutal brawling of the Nazis. Not one. What, then, ailed these men who had been his friends? They had no civic or moral courage. They huddled in the apparent security of an unfeatured and coagulated mass; they sought a degraded refuge in an undifferentiated mob. They ceased to be free personalities and were just good enough to be the cannon fodder of their new masters. *That* is the supreme danger which faces our society as well.

But an even more striking example can be adduced. On January 7, 1918, Lenin dispersed the duly elected Constituent Assembly at the point of the bayonet. The dictatorship thus established at once exhibited the blood-drenched ruthlessness of every dictatorship. The intellectuals and the middle class were starved and tortured to death. Their children were excluded from the schools. Young Jews were forced to denounce their parents and grandparents as counter-revolutionaries and thus condemn them to a painful death. The mass murder of all dissidents set in at once. Horrors were piled on horrors. The Soviet slave state was unashamedly in the making. Yet all over the Western World and not least in America and not least among young Jews in America, men and women became the passionate defenders of that rule by whip and scourge and torture and death in its foulest forms, as though they, too, lusted after that extinction of the free and self-sustaining personality and wanted to merge their own being in a clotted and unfeatured mass.

All through the third and almost through the fourth decades of this century the moral and spiritual degradation of these attitudes continued. The awakening in regard to Soviet Russia has been rude and almost universal. But the attitudes which made possible that partisanship of tyranny and obliteration in the mass, have not wholly disappeared.

We prate of freedom and do not use it; we congratulate ourselves on living in a libertarian society and act like slaves. Younger Jews, older Jews, urged toward spiritual self-realization and toward the exercise of their American freedom, shiver at the thought of their destined differentiation and make gestures of propitiation toward a notion of a mass society, a "crowd culture" which, by this self-degradation they help to intensify. If ever, which may God forbid, America were to demand of its citizens that they be spiritual slaves, uniformed robots, those Jews who today refuse their destiny and their Jewish integrity will have contributed to that evil end.

How does that fear of freedom manifest itself? Primarily by the use of certain verbal rubber-stamps. For instance: intensive Jewish education is proposed and a word is flung at the proponent. The word is "segregation." Or Jews establish a university. From certain quarters comes the strange word "ghettoization." But Jews *exist*. They exist, as was said long ago, as an historic group of recognizable homogeneity. Differentiated existence is in itself segregation. It is segregation by the fiat of nature or of God. Whoever, whether individual or group, seeks flight from his or its destined segregation, evidently seeks obliteration or death.

The word "segregation" will repay scrutiny. It means withdrawal of *se* (oneself) from the *grex* the herd, the merely *gre*garious mass). Now every civilized act is an act of differentiation, of segregation. Going to college, reading authentic literature, hearing sound music — any and all such acts are acts of separation from the mass. And these acts and all similar acts become more and more necessary and precious, if we would have civilization endure at all.

Many years ago that scrupulous thinker, Paul Valéry, expressed his anguished apprehension that the attempt to diffuse culture through ever widening masses would mean its degradation and, perhaps, extinction. His fears, as everyone knows who permits himself to observe and think at all, have been all but fulfilled.

Nor has this catastrophe been unnoticed in America. The voices of older men (Bernard Iddings Bell: "Crowd Culture",) and of younger men (Peter Viereck: "Conservatism Revisited") have in anguished accents marked and denounced the fatal submergence of qualitative by quantitative valuations, the reduction of all educational and cultural activities to the broadest and hence most undifferentiated common denominator, the consequent obliteration of personality, of personal values, of choice and the very ability to choose and so, in the last analysis, of freedom itself.

It has been at last perceived, in other words, that democracy by reducing itself to the absurd, by stigmatising any hierarchy or rank of values as undemocratic, by resisting *distinction* and *distinguishedness* themselves, can dig its own grave, can sink into a totalitarian morass.

13

In a society so menaced the act or fact of segregation, whether dictated by an historical destiny or in pursuit of an intelligible ideal, has a better chance of being good and fruitful and moral than almost any other human trend or act. He who has an historic separateness dictated by a great tradition and seeks to obliterate it, to throw it off, to destroy his segregation and merge himself into the *grex*, the herd, the mob, may not unjustly be called a traitor to the cause of the Western spirit, of those great traditions which must be saved if we are not to sink into barbarism. The intensity of a Jew's Jewishness is the measure of his service to this civilization in which we live.

TRADITION AND ITS MEANING

At this point a brief recapitulation may be in place. If today, here in America, you are known as a Jew and know yourself to be one, you are faced by an objective existential fact that is unescapable. What you will subjectively *do* with that objective fact will determine your character as a Jew, a human being, a citizen. Affirming and intensifying what you inevitably are, integrating your intellectual life and your life within society about your Jewish centrality, will be your best service to your spiritual development as well as to the society and culture of which you are a part.

If this argument is persuasive, the next question

that arises is the question: by what instrumentality is this integration about a Jewish centrality to be accomplished? To this question there is but one answer: The instrumentality is the individual's absorption of and into the totality of the historic tradition of the Jewish people.

Tradition! The word has been repeatedly used here, not without an awareness of the fact that it has, in recent decades, fallen into a measure of disrepute. Younger people, older people, have been heard to say: "But that is *only* traditional!" Or: "That is a mere following of tradition!" Or: "Why should I conform to tradition?"

Once more we have a word, the word "tradition", which is worth close scrutiny. *Tradere* is a Latin verb which means to hand down, to transmit, bequeath, instruct. The matter handed down or bequeathed or taught by parent to child, by teacher to pupil is the *traditio* of the culture in which that parent and child, that teacher and pupil exist. Without tradition there would be no continuity and no culture, even the humblest. If every human being had to invent for himself the arts of civilization, or speech or morals or even manners; if there were no conventions or agreements concerning either the ascertained or the preferable, there would be no civilization. If each generation could not assume what was handed down through the preceding generations there would be no continuity, nor order, nor such progress as there has been. Memory, as the Greeks said, is in truth the mother of all the Muses. The memories of the race are the substance of history. The whole purpose of a liberal education is to make the student the partaker of that substance. He whose mind has no past is an empty creature. He whose mind has no past cannot build upon what has been and must start feebly and blankly on an empty barbarism.

We can see all about us how the neglect of the humanistic and historic and memoried tradition has created those barbaric mobs who flock to the standards of the dictator, the rabble-rouser, the vociferous fool. The modern poet, as T. S. Eliot has so admirably said, knows more than the masters of old. It is *their* works that constitute his increase in knowledge. We, too, *may* know more than our fathers knew by virtue of our possession of the knowledge and wisdom which *they* accumulated for us. Tradition is our foundation; without it we are as nothing. From it *alone* we can go forth.

We can go forth! For tradition need not be fixed and final. It is cumulative and flexible. But in order to add to it or to change it, one must first know it. What would one say, to take the humblest example, of a man setting out to invent a machine without a knowledge of the principles of mechanics or a knowledge of what had been done in his field? A nuclear physicist advancing into the dire infinitudes of his science must have mastered all that is known and has been discovered and even surmised.

In the field of faith and morals, of history and law, we, too, must know before we can add or change.

There has been no more discouraging phenomenon in contemporary Jewish life than those younger or older intellectuals who pretended to themselves to desire to return to their Judaism and their Jewishness and refused, first of all, to absorb and be absorbed by that immortal tradition, that vast and poignant body of thought, of aspiration, of knowledge, of wisdom, which our fathers experienced, created out of their great experiences, and recorded for us.

Is it clear now that the instrumentality by which the right subjective use of the objective fact of one's Jewishness can be made, is by the absorption of and into that mighty stream of Jewish tradition, that Torah, that directive and teaching in its broadest sense, to which, according to a famous saying of our sages, every devout and devoted Jew can validly *add* the interpretation of his generation and of his day.

But he cannot re-interpret what he does not know. Nor can he add to tradition which he has not mastered. He cannot teach a new aspect of Jewish history, Jewish wisdom, Jewish aspiration to his children or pupils until he is in possession of what has been and what is.

Let us then clear our minds of that silly, derogatory attitude toward tradition. Let us ask ourselves, if we can — it will not be easy — what is the character and what is the content of that Jewish historic experience, incarnated in the tradition which is the instrumentality needed today by Jews to make of their objective, their existential Jewishness, the central spiritual factor of their lives.

THE HERITAGE: ITS FORM

It is hard and it is wrong in any matter to divide substance from form, content from outer manifestation. But it is often convenient and occasionally illuminating. We must be on our guard not to forget that substance and form are in reality like the obverse and the reverse of a coin. If you slice the coin through the middle it has neither meaning nor value. But you may look first at one side and next at the other. From these views a synthesis may be obtained.

Let us look at the form, the outer manisfestation of Jewish history. It has three strange characteristics: the first is its *endurance* or length. The second is its *recurrence*. The third (which is a direct consequence of the second) is its *ever-presentness* in and to each generation. Let us look at these three characteristics in order.

I

Let us confine ourselves for the moment to the hard facts of secular history, to the ascertainable and ascertained. The tribally united *B'nei Yisrael*, the children of Israel, took possession of Cana'an and settled in the land in (roughly) 1250 before the Common Era. This occurrence, namely, the conquest of Cana'an by Joshua bin Nun and the men of Israel, has its world-wide analogues. Aryan-speaking peoples came from the North and conquered the Indian sub-continent and stamped it as their own; Hellenic tribes came from the East and took possession of the lands of which they were to make Hellas or Greece; Angles and Saxons invaded Celtic Britain which then became forever England.

Neither the Torah nor the Prophetic books of Israel nor Homer nor the plays of Sophocles nor the works of Chaucer or Shakespeare or Milton were written by the ultimate aborigines of the lands that gave them birth. They were all written by conquerors who transformed Cana'an into Eretz Yisrael, the land of Israel; the easternmost peninsula and islands of Europe into Hellas; and Britain into England.

Thus the beginning of Israel's secular history conforms to a pattern not unknown or unfamiliar. But the 3303 years that have elapsed since the walls of Jericho fell, seeing that modern archaeology has proven their fall, present a quite other and quite abnormal spectacle. The commonwealth or state or kingdom or kingdoms established by the children of Israel was, from the time of the Judges on to its final extinction by Rome, a strange and an unquiet one. This particular people disliked and feared governmental authority from the start. It yearned for the rulership of God; it was frightened of the idolatry of the state from its most primitive period on.

The story of Gideon, the fable of Jotham in the Book of Judges, bear incontrovertible evidence of that fear. If there were to be a king he was to be stripped of power and splendor; his constitution was to be the Torah, the directive of God. When the people wrung the institution of kingship from the reluctant judge and prophet, the kings did not, of course, conform to this ideal. Hence the kings, from Saul on, were kings beset by an evil conscience. They bowed down before the accusing prophets, from Nathan on; or else, like Solomon, they built the Temple or gave it their support.

Powerful empires threatened this small, turbulent people with its troubled conscience. When Babylon conquered it and destroyed both Jerusalem and the Temple and deported (note the aptness of that modern term) the majority of the inhabitants of the land of Israel to strange places, that should normally have ended its history. Here then we have the first great deviation and here the first unconscious aspiration toward perpetuity. Not all the Israelites in Babylon retained character, faith, sense of destiny. Not all. But a core and remnant did here, as it has done everywhere and always, so that when Cyrus the Persian permitted the return of the exiles, there was a people ready to return; there was a scribe and prophet, Ezra, ready to lead them to return; there were those ready to rebuild the Temple, trowel in one hand, sword in the other, even as the sons of Israel rebuilt the broken land into a State, while fighting off the Arab armies in our own immediate day.

It is difficult, clearly, to keep the theme of endurance, of perpetuity, disentangled from the theme of *recurrence*. Babylon was only the first mighty threat to the existence of Israel. Hellenistic civilization, comparable to the brilliant civilizations of Europe and America in modern times, sought to engulf and destroy the very being of the Jewish people. Again a remnant resisted and fought and won the Maccabean victory. And last in antiquity came Rome, which could endure to shelter all other subject peoples and religions under her peace, only not the Jews and their Temple, only not this small people with a troubled conscience and with its fear of the state and of idolatry. And so in almost seventy years of war it fought this people down and decimated it and drove it from its land and caused the price of a Jewish slave on the market-places of the empire to be less than the price of a horse.

Should this not have been the end? At this point, on the contrary, the uniqueness of the Jewish historical experience becomes luminously manifest. Troy was annihilated. We hear no more of the Trojans save in the palpable Vergilian legend. The Jews survived the destruction of their fatherland. They became homeless wanderers, perpetual minority groups within triumphant and hostile states and cultures, harried and decimated again and again — during the Crusades (which also destroyed the last feeble footholds in the Land of Israel), in the times of the Black Death in Central Europe, during the Ukrainian uprisings in the seventeenth Century — on and on — to the Germanic pagan fury of our own day which tortured to death almost one half of the living Jewish people, up to that slow spiritual attrition practiced by the Soviets and culminating almost on the day on which these lines are written by the unleashed fury of the trials in Prague.

Yet we are here!

Jews are here. And we are more than merely here. The establishment of the State of Israel; the consolidation of the great American Jewish Community, of which this essay is a small sign and symbol; the intensification of Jewish life in other, smaller corners of the wide dispersion — all these phenomena bear witness to the unique perpetuity and will to live of the people Israel.

II

It has already been said how hard it is to keep apart the survival of the Jewish people from the recurrences of Jewish history. But it may be clear by now that Jews survived attacks that were always identical in ultimate motivation, however various they seemed in the rationalizations behind which the evil conscience of the world withdrew. From Cicero and the Alexandrian anti-Semites, concerning whom Josephus reports, on to the neo-Pagan butcheries and deportations of the Twentieth Century, the ultimate motivation of attack against the Jewish people was one and the same: to eliminate that threat and reproach to the world's inveterate pagan instincts which the very existence of the Jew embodies and incarnates.

Even the formula scarcely changes. "If the Jews are Alexandrian citizens," asked that Apion against whom so long ago Josephus wrote, "why do they not worship the gods of the city?" The worshippers of the one transcendent God could not ever worship the idols of any city, any *polis*, any state, neither of Alexandria nor of Rome, neither of the mediaeval empires nor of the contemporary ones.

Therefore, from Apion of Alexandria to Lenin the attempts, whether by persuasion or menace, were always the same: to force Jews into the idolatry of the gods of a particular city. Lenin wrote as early as 1913:

> "Half the Jews live under conditions favoring maximum assimilation . . . Jewish national culture is the slogan of rabbis and bourgeois . . . Jewish Marxists who merge with Russians, Lithuanians, Ukrainians contribute their share."

Assimilation here, as nearly everywhere, does not mean a reasonable sharing of the cultures of the peoples among whom Jews dwell. It means worshipping the idols of the city. It means the extinction of Jewish identity. But the Jewish people has not been able to will deliberate extinction in the mire of the Pagan world. Hitler perhaps saw that most clearly and therefore attempted the last resort of physical obliteration. And that, too, failed.

Thus nothing new ever happens to Jews. The new things are illusory.

Our civic emancipation was to eliminate the Jewish problem. It brought forth other phenomena of the intensification of that problem. Nor was that all. It subtly turned the attack inward and began to gnaw away the spiritual substance of the Jewish people. And so, for the first time in history, there began to appear Jews who, though sharing all aspects of Jewish destiny, began to lose knowledge of and faith in the inner and eternal reasons; they became Jewish anti-semites and began to declare that Jews survived only by virtue of the recurrence of anti-semitism, forgetting the glaring fact that, had Jews been able wholly to disappear, anti-semitism could not have survived. The one thing it needs to feed on is Jews, living and recognizable.

Hence it is clear that it is the destined and inextinguishable Jewish will to live that forever re-evokes the resistance of the fury of the Pagans and their rebellion against God and good. Thus it comes about that whenever that fury re-arises the deluded wanderers of the house of Israel return to the core and matrix of their people. And they return, like the eminent philosopher Henri Bergson so recently, not slinkingly, not shame-facedly, not with gloom but with a liberating incandescence in their proud, tragic and repentant hearts.

III

Now it will perhaps be understood how the involuntary persistence of the Jewish people and the recurrences in Jewish history which are due to the ultimate reasons for that people's endurance, cause all of Jewish history to be present in the Jewish mind. We understand the story of the assimilated Moses smiting the cruel Egyptian task-master of his people, because we know how the assimilated Theodore Herzl saw the pagans smite Alfred Dreyfus. Moses fled into the desert to lead his people. And so did Herzl. And even as from this act and flight of Moses came the exodus and the liberation, so from the act and flight of Herzl came, in our people's direst need, the exodus and liberation of the State of Israel.

Is it any wonder, then, that authentic Jews speak of Moses as the great present and eternal symbol of a people's recurrent enslavement and liberation? You can go through the stories of the Torah, the five Books of Moses, and through the tales of the historical books of our Scripture and through the lives and sayings of the Prophets and you may, if you like (though this is *not* the view of the present writer) regard all that you read as poetic and symbolic. And thereupon, surveying the Jewish events of your own immediate day in all their tragic weight as well as in all their subtlest intricacies, you will find them all pre-figured, all narrated, all foreshadowed and foretold.

Jewish history has a singular unity of *form*. This unity of form leaps to the eye from nearly every page of the liturgy. The old, old penitential poems of the persecuted were written once more in our own day by a stylistically ultra-modern poet named Karl

Wolfskehl; the congregation of Israel prayed throughout the ages that it might be able to establish its freedom (*cherut* — freedom) by the ingathering of its exiles from the four corners of the earth to bring them back — as the State of Israel has done and is doing — to Zion. And when in the Passover ritual, the Pesach Hagadah, we read: "In every generation they rise against us, and in every generation the Holy One, Blessed be He, delivers us out of their hands," we know — we who have witnessed, all of us, the old and the young, the death-camps and the crematoriums, and who are witnessing now the outbreak of the long-smouldering Russian fury — we know that we are speaking not only of things far and remote but of things immediate and burning in their deadly reality.

Egypt and Rome and the Crusaders and the Pagan empires of today all blend into a strange simultaneity of which the character and outcome were foretold in that scripture which is the immortal transcript of both our character and our destiny.

Now there are deluded and self-deluded people who imagine vainly that this long continuity of Jewish history can be broken; that its recurrence can be ended and its unity destroyed. They pretend to themselves — as did many German Jews and many French Jews between, say, 1848 and 1930 — that anti-semitism can be eliminated by education, by psychological analysis, by sociological devices. They spend millions of dollars on this task and doubtless they are sincere and honest men and equally doubtless they can, in a reasonably free society, mitigate the cruder manifestations of anti-Semitism amid the crack-brained mob. But its roots cannot be plucked out by any devices which such people use, for the simple reason — simple but massive — that the use of these devices betrays a wholly false notion of what anti-Semitism is. Today and here its loud manifestations are almost, though not wholly, confined to a frustrated rabble. But let us not forget that the literature of the English tongue, from Chaucer's "Prioress's Tale" through Marlowe's "Jew of Malta" to Aldous Huxley and T. S. Eliot and Ezra Pound is immitigably anti-semitic. It is so out of a defensive instinct; it is so as a gesture of avoidance and exculpation; it is so because anti-semitism is the mark and sign and symbol of an unredeemed world.

Unfathomably profound was the prayer of one of the masters of the Hasidic movement, the Maggid or preacher of Kosnitz. "Lord of the Universe," the Kosnitzer prayed, "if thou wouldst not redeem the Jews, redeem the *goyim*, the gentiles." If the world's peoples were redeemed, if they practiced the Jewish ethic taught by Jesus of Nazareth, the Jew would no longer be felt to be nay-sayer, adversary, incarnate reproach and sting of conscience.

It was no accident that the German so-called higher criticism of the Bible sought to undermine the authenticity and historicity of the Hebrew scriptures in order ultimately to undermine that scripture as the foundation of the Christian teachings.

When the Hitlerian murderers declared Christianity to be a foul, oriental superstition imposed upon the blond barbarians of the North, that long undermining appeared in its true colours. Murder and rapine were now no longer sins. The law of God was abrogated.

When the Bolsheviks turned churches into Atheists' clubs and synagogues into hog-butcheries and of all the languages known to man forbade the study and teaching of Hebrew alone, they hoisted the same pagan banner and could proceed calmly to the "liquidation" of all deviationists of all kinds and build their economic structure on the basis of untold millions of slaves. So once again arose a Pharaonic tyrant and idol.

So long as Pharaoh is re-embodied, whether his name be Hitler or Stalin; so long as even in free societies, money and power are kings; so long as God's law — thou shalt not worship idols nor kill nor steal — is subordinated wholly to greed and blood and lust for power — so long must anti-semitism persist, mildly in democratic pseudo-Christian states, furiously where even lip-worship of God has ceased and the Pharaoh-Caesar-State is once more the idol whom Jews cannot and will not worship. And a Jew who casts aside his heritage and merges with the Pagan world and worships its idols, does not only betray himself but prevents, in the measure of his power, the redemption of that world with which he has made his wretched peace.

THE HERITAGE: ITS CONTENT

Perhaps it is clear now what is the form of Jewish history and destiny, the form of the Jewish heritage to any one who is known as a Jew and knows himself to be one. And this *form* has been for mere convenience treated alone and something has been said concerning the delusions of those who do not even grasp the configuration of that form. But form and content are undivided and indivisible, as mind and body are, and have a single impact, even as a work of art has a single impact and is to be analysed into its several aspects only at both the critic's and the artist's peril.

Let us however once more say for convenience that the content of the Jewish heritage shaped the form of Jewish history. What precisely was it that caused Jews to persist against the storm of the ages; what was it that evoked those storms; what, then, caused the recurrence and perpetual presentness of Jewish history and the Jewish heritage.

There are two kinds of causes; proximate and ultimate — the near and immediate and the last and final. And it is hard to answer any truly important question in this immediate age in terms of final and ultimate causes because there exists an antecedent prejudice against them. This prejudice is very powerful in contemporary America. Most children, both Jews and Christians, attend the public schools during the most plastic years of their lives. Now the religion of the public schools is, according to the correct definition of Canon Bernard Iddings Bell, "a non-theistic and merely patriotic Secularism." Cultural attitudes are determined there; prejudices are created there. A youth will think it "smart" in the double sense of clever and fashionable to declare himself an "agnostic"; in the age of Planck and Einstein he will talk about religion and science in terms of the age of Haeckel and Huxley. Political and economic questions will commonly be tinged with a shade of "pink". By subtle implication, at least, the Soviet Slave State will be represented as a phase, however clouded, of man's struggle for a just society.

Amid such brutal, withered and reactionary fallacies children grow into adolescents and into adult status enmeshed in a web of superstitions that are much farther from the realities of man's true life than were the superstitions of the so-called ages of faith. Nor is this all. Many "liberal" clergymen and many "liberal" rabbis also unfortunately cultivate the latest intellectual fashions of sixty years ago and when extolling, properly enough, the human reason, forget the great dictum of Kant that one of the supreme functions of the reason is to understand and define its own limitations.

On such terms the content of the Jewish heritage cannot be grasped. That "non-theistic and merely patriotic Secularism" which constitutes the primary cultural assumption of the American public school system is a patent form of that idolatry which Jews of all ages have refused in life and death. It is a form of that idolatry of nature or man himself or of the state which, as every living soul who has witnessed the rise of Hitler and of Stalin should know by immediate experience, is the last and most immitigable of evils.

For *if* there is no unshatterable Law that is above all laws; or — take which formulation you prefer — if our values are not transcendentally validated — there is no reason (nor anything in man's unassisted reason) to prevent you from feeding your fellowmen (including 1,100,000 children) into crematoriums yesterday or working and starving them to death in slave-kennels today. There is (let us search our minds in all fairness) *no* compelling reason. Once more it will be fruitful to cite one of the most rigorous thinkers, one of the most responsible writers (neither a Christian nor a Jew, by the way) of our time. In his magnificent last book (*L'homme révolté*, "Man in Revolt",) Albert Camus writes:

> "If one believes in nothing, if nothing has any meaning, and if we can affirm no value, everything is possible and nothing has any importance. There is no argument for or against anything and the assassin is neither wrong nor right. You can build crematoriums or devote yourself to nursing lepers. Malevolence and virtue are matters of chance or whim."

Therefore — the chain of reasoning here is strict — the primary content of the Jewish heritage is formulated in the commandment: "Thou shalt have no other gods before me." The Jewish people emerged from the general Semitic matrix when Abram (call it history or, if you must, appropriate poetic symbol) discovered the One God and made a Covenant with him. That Covenant, that *B'rith*, which symbolically is renewed by every Jewish man-child, constitutes also the discovery of the free human personality. For only a free and self-sustaining human personality — no slave-soul or state-slave or mere conformer without will — can make a Covenant with God. Here, first, man took upon himself the worship of the Highest and chose to obey that Highest, the unique, unalterable God and His law.

No wonder that the sages of the Talmud poetically fancied that Abraham obeyed the entire Law by prophetic intuition, even though it was not given from Sinai until centuries later. For indeed, as the whole trend of history demonstrates, there is no curb upon human evil, nor any limit to it, unless the One God alone is worshipped and not the idols of wood or stone or a Leader or a State or a philosophic Absolute.

The Jewish people, then, emerged from the Semitic matrix and from the matrix of general history by first and alone and uniquely saying: NO — *NO* — to the idolatry of the world. For this NO is the deepest implication of the recognition of the One God and of the integrated human personality which freely chooses to worship that One God and refuses to bow down to idols.

In brief, this negation is implied in that vast and immortal affirmation which is the ultimate substance of the Jewish heritage: "Hear, O Israel, the Lord our God is One."

With these words upon his lips every authentic Jew breathes his last. With these words upon their lips our martyrs went to their death in Rome and Spain, in Germany and Poland. And this essay has been written in vain if it is not already supremely clear that the "Hear, O Israel . . ." is not a magic or mystic formula, but a declaration of the one and unique possibility of human redemption from evil — the worship of the One God, the obedience to His law, the refusal to bow down to the idols and to obey their laws.

The discovery of Abraham was consolidated and elaborated at the foot of Sinai by his descendants who — we are now on the firm ground of history — became a people, this people to which every Jew belongs here and today by receiving (or, if you prefer creating) the Law of God in its entirety, a Law for Jew and a Noachide Law for non-Jew. A Law for man. A law that centers around the refusal of idolatry. A Law that has made it impossible for the Jew to worship and bow down "to the gods of the city", of any city, of any state, seeing that all these gods are idols — not to the idols of Rome nor of Constantine nor of the emerging secular, merely nationalistic states of modern times, nor to the idols of Hitler or of Stalin.

That central affirmation of the Oneness and

Uniqueness of God with its implication of an eternal NO to the idolatries of the Pagans — this is the core of the Jewish heritage, this is the core of the resistance which an unredeemed world has offered from age to age to the very existence of the Jewish people.

An immediate corollary must again be added: any Jew who, in the face of these tremendous facts of all experience, ceases by all he is to practice that affirmation and its implied negation, has no further reason for existence. Though biologically alive he is a dead soul. He has despaired not only of himself and his people. He has despaired of mankind or of any hope for mankind.

THE CLASSICAL FOUNDATION

The core and center of the content of the Jewish heritage has now been defined. But it has been merely defined. Now man cannot and does not live by an articulated definition or idea. The Jewish tradition and the Jewish heritage have been incarnated; they have been lived by; they have been died for in all ages. They have created and consist of a vast and complete culture. The Jewish people created this culture and was, in turn, shaped by it. This culture in its recorded form preserved the Jewish people as a living people in half the lands of earth when it had lost soil and city and state and should, by all the experience of all other peoples, have disappeared.

From time to time the Jewish creative spirit seemed to burn low and to be near extinction. Each time a luminous re-birth set in.

Thus in the eighteenth century in Eastern Europe arose the Hasidic movement and the Hasidic way, of which the living evangels and the ever-living *Zaddikim* or wholly consecrated souls, are among the chief products of man's religious and ethical genius.

Thus, toward the end of the nineteenth century, amid the bitter disappointments of the so-called emancipation, there arose the Lovers of Zion in the East and Herzl and his comrades in the West, and that process of the redemption of the soil of the land of Israel for the redemption of the people set in. It produced a great literature and, as action, culminated in the proclamation of the State of Israel in 1948 and in the ingathering of the exiles from the four corners of the earth.

Thus, too, from amid the extreme assimilationists of Germany and Austria, there arose, after the first World War, that radiant re-birth of Judaism which is rightly associated with the names of Franz Rosenzweig and Martin Buber. To their feet and to their Houses of Learning, under the shadow of ultimate tragedy, there came the Jewish youth who had been almost lost among the idolaters of the world and recovered and re-lived and re-incarnated the immemorial and ever-living and ever-new tradition, the heritage, the faith and form.

Thus the young Jew in America today inherits a tradition not only of antiquity, but as it has been reborn, relived, re-incarnated in the modern era.

These modern examples have been adduced first in order to make it quite clear that the Jewish heritage is one of a burning and ever-renewed life. Survivors of the ghettos of Vilna and Warsaw have created a new school of Yiddish poetry. Had Segalowitch written in Gaelic, let us say; were Avram Sutzkever writing in Danish, the "little magazines" would long ago have discovered them, as they would also have discovered the masters of neo-Hebrew literature, from Agnon to Yitzchak Schenberg.

In every one of its great deaths the Jewish people has flowered into new life; from every one of its graves it has experienced a resurrection. And the quite conventional anti-semite in the person of Toynbee calls this living people a "fragment of a fossil of Syriac society"!

Now all these movements of the Jewish people's rebirth from age to age have conformed to a pattern which is more or less the pattern created by all cultural forces. The simplest single word for this pattern is separation. Separation, differentiation, the development from homogeneity to heterogeneity — is not that the process and aim of all civilization? Is not the lifting of the free and differentiated personality out of the clotted mob almost the chief aim by which man can become human?

So people, too, separates itself from people, ethnic group from ethnic group, by language, rhythm, sensibility, a special reaction toward "man and nature and human life". Thus first with Abraham and later at Sinai the Jewish people separated itself from all the other peoples and remained separate, even as each people remains separate, but with an additional separateness from all of the world's peoples by virtue of that immortal affirmation of the One God's oneness and the implicit negation of the world's idolatries.

But the Jewish people, though never wholly losing sight of its character and redemptive function for man, was a very human people and often, as we know from the Prophets on to this very day, forsook its God and its calling and went whoring after the idols of the pagan world. The inner history of Israel is often the history of apostasy and return. Kings did evil; the priesthood in a late age became Hellenized and sought to merge the people with the world and so destroy its being and its function.

Thus priesthood and Temple and the sacrificial cult yielded in preeminence to the synagogue which was then, as it is now, a people's house, a house of prayer and, perhaps above all, a house of study.

They who effected this final separation and revolution in Jewish life; they who — with roots of tradition going back to Ezra and the return from Babylon — laid the foundations of classical Judaism, the Judaism of the ages and the Judaism of today, were those men whom the Christian Gospels call the Pharisees. Now the word Pharisees is the Hellenized form of the Hebrew word *Perushim*, which means: the separated ones. We read of a certain sage, Yehuda, the son of Durtai, that he separated himself (*peresh*), he and his son and went forth to dwell in the South. And it is but the other day that, in Eastern Europe, before the days of the great martyrdom, young men left house and home and kin, separating themselves from the world, in order to study, to practice *perishut*, separatedness for the sake of holiness, for the sake of perfection. The separation from the world thus practiced is never a surly or contemptuous one. Holiness or perfection is to be gained for the sake of that very world from which separation is effected. Its aim is the redemption of that very world.

Does that sound very odd in the ears of youth in America in 1954? Does not everyone rush, as though the earth were on fire under his feet, to merge and blend with the contemporary world, to be "normal", to "conform", to become stupidly confined to one language and a single literature, to want and need redemption at the very bottom of one's heart and to deny that even to oneself and run after the substitutes, the *ersatz* of counting noses and sending out questionnaires and all the other hocus-pocus of the so-called Social Sciences?

Do you bear the same love toward your neighbor as toward yourself, as the eternal Law bids? No, you take a course in Social Relations. Do you withdraw to meditate upon some great creation of the human spirit in separatedness, in tranquility, or do you run to hear a lecture and engage in a discussion? Are you surprised that psycho-therapeutics are so widely needed and therefore so widely practiced? When you take courses in psychology, how often do you do so out of an inner anxiety and restlessness and dividedness which, according to a faint hope, this study may allay and how often do you do so from an interest in psychology as an objective science?

This age in which we live has been called the "age of anxiety", and such it is. In your own time two pagan rebellions have arisen — the National Socialist or Nazi rebellion and the Communist or Soviet rebellion — against all the traditions, laws, compacts, sanctities of Western man. They have instigated the cruelest wars — the hot wars and the cold wars — of all history. But that is not all. They have practiced a cruelty of man to man, a cruelty of which the Jews have been only the most conspicuous and significant victims, which surpasses in its icy fury all the cruelties and all the horrors of all the barbarians of the past. And the excellent people who sit in the United Nations Assembly propose a "resolution" against "genocide."

Well, the Nazis resolved on a new order and murdered all possible dissidents; the Soviets resolved on a new order and are still murdering all dissidents. Any movement is bound to win for the time being, if all who disagree are murdered. But this method or an approach to this method of the "proscription" of the dissidents by those in power, of the ins by the outs, is bound to prevail, if all the sources of social change are sought within society itself, that is, if a certain portion of society, ambitious men, corrupt men, cruel men, declare their "truth" to be "*the* truth", to be an absolute in the name of which all ethical limitations can be scrapped. To pursue this course both the Nazis and the Communists had first to curse and outlaw God and the Law of God, all separateness and separation from the mere social order, all values which transcend that social order and by which it and its devices may be judged.

This, this precisely, is the cause of the anxiety which gnaws at every heart. Outer security is a secondary matter. Man has, upon the whole, a certain brute physical courage. It is all inner security that is gone by reason of a total submersion within social forces, an almost total abandonment of those transcendent principles by which social forces are to be judged and guided. If the mark of Cain is no longer a physical and a metaphysical stigma, who shall not fear?

Jews are the *Perushim*, the separated ones. Therefore are they considered enemies and poisoners by the pagan barbarians. Jews are those who regard society and its forces from without, from an eternal point of vantage, from (literally or symbolically) an everlasting Sinai. They have heard (literally or symbolically) the promulgation of the only Law by which man can be redeemed. Therefore — it cannot be repeated too often — any Jew who closes his ear to that Law which once upon a time his fathers heard and passed on to him, any Jew who seeks to forget that Law and merges with any pagan community, merges uncritically with any merely temporal society, has no function and no reason-for-being left him. Thus being a Jew consciously, absorbedly, affirmatively is for him the ultimate existential problem. He is separate by the fiat of history and destiny. He must assent to his separateness to give meaning to his life.

THE PATH TO TREAD

The process of regaining this necessary assent to his separateness is not a simple or easy one for the Jew who has lost his way amid the blinding glare and the real enough splendors of the Pagan world. Beauty is there and that beauty is in truth his to share and to dwell with. But has not that world shown, especially in this age, as in no other, its total failure in wisdom and righteousness, its total impotence not to be submerged in blood and mire? Of what avail is beauty, if it is doomed to extinction in war and degradation? We know now, as the great French critic and poet Paul Valéry wrote a score of years ago, that Keats and Baudelaire can be submerged in waves of barbarism, even as were Menander and his fellows.

The Jew's ancestral commitment to the only Law

that can save man, to the only way that can redeem the world, must be renewed by his total active re-commitment to his Judaism. If he does not so re-commit himself he is but half a man; he is but a cripple and a divided soul. His station within history is spiritually determined. If he abandons this station his innermost consciousness will know — however much he twist and turn and rationalize — that he has betrayed the flag of redemption in the very face of the implacable barbarian enemy.

Our fathers were divinely fortunate. They did not have to reason this matter out. They knew. They pursued the Jewish way which separated it-self from the ways of the unredeemed world and said "No" to that world. But we later generations have let the pagan world's resistance to redemption insinuate itself into our souls. Young Jews pose as unfeatured "liberals"; they babble about mere changes in social techniques and forget — as Jews should never forget — that the old unredeemed men in the new social techniques will not have become re-deemed. No, the new social techniques only serve to free them from traditional restraints, so that unheard of depths of horror are opened by *Gauleiter* and *Commissar*.

We must find our way back. The individual Jew, the young Jew of today must find his way back. In the beginning there must be the moral re-commitment. There must be a deep sense of the world's woe and of the centrality of the historic position of the Jewish people within the only redemptive forces which the world has known. We gave the world Christianity; we gave the world Islam. The redemptive Jewish elements in both of the daughter religions are being abandoned. Hence the world slides back into chaos. We must not lower the torch. Such is the groundwork of Jewish re-commitment.

But this re-commitment cannot suffice if it is merely a matter of information and principle, if it remains an intellectual attitude. A life is to be lived and a way to be pursued, an exemplary life and a way of redemption. Principles are of value only if they are woven into a texture of living. *Halacha* means the Way, even as the Chinese *Tao* means the way, even as Jesus of Nazareth said that his Way (an essentially Jewish and Pharasaic Way) was the Way.

That Way which Jews have pursued, that *Halacha* is the way of the sanctification of all life, in order that life may be truly human and may illustrate man's likeness to God. It is a way of separateness from the ways of the Pagans and must be so for the very Pagans' sake. The Jew's re-commitment is not a re-commitment of preaching or teaching, of writing or joining parties. It is a vitalistic matter. It is a life to be lived. And it is to be lived not consciously or spectacularly but with quiet self-containment, with tranquility, with dignity, beyond all striving and crying and clamor and contention.

This life cannot, of course, be lived in isolation and alone. It is to be lived within the historic community of eternal Israel, but is to be activated within the living community of one's own day.

A Jew, a young Jew, who desires to re-commit himself to his true destiny, cannot separate himself from the fellowship of Israel in the concrete here and now. The nearest synagogue may not seem aglow with the *Shechinah*, the Abiding within it of the Divine. It is to be remembered that we have, with the rest of mankind, "fallen upon evil days and evil tongues, by danger and by darkness compassed round", as Milton said so long ago. Perhaps you, humble and alone, are destined in your maturity to bring back a living spark of what is now so often only a memory or an aspiration. But if you, within an, after all, living community, begin again to practice such *mitzvot*, such good commanded deeds as, within your limitations, you can practice; if the love of Israel and the understanding of its destiny once more make Torah and the sanctification commanded by Torah dear to your heart — if the Halacha, the Way, seems a good and beautiful way to you once more, then it is *your* return from alienation which will bring nearer, according to a Talmudic image, the slow dawn of the redemption of Israel.

A well-known Talmudic anecdote has it that a group of sages debated: what is more precious: Torah (study) or righteous action? The first impulse of the sages was, of course, to prefer righteous action, for Judaism is a religion of righteousness. A second thought decided that Torah was more important, since only from Torah could the rightness of an action and the rightness of the inner intention of an action be learned.

It is clear, then, how the young Jew of today is to find his way back to a Jewish creative life. Fortunately for him the great spiritual wealth of the Jewish people is written in *Torah*, Torah in its widest sense of the complete body of recorded Jewish experience, from the scriptures on to the works of Martin Buber, who still lives in Jerusalem, and to the works of men still young and still adding to our permanent wealth. And nearly that entire record is now available in the English language.

Is it, then, a matter of reading books? Not wholly. There is scarcely an American Jewish community today in which there does not live a true and learned teacher in Israel. It may not be the Rabbi whom you happen to know. It may be a Hebrew teacher; it may be a learned layman, a *lamdan*, to use the classical term. It may be a quite humble person who, by his learning and by his life illustrates not only the knowledge of Torah but, according to the Hassidic ideal, the *being* of Torah. And there is assuredly hardly a college or university in America today that has not such a one on its faculty or in its immediate neighborhood. So, by all means, choose yourself a teacher.

But reading is still both fundamental and essential. And what, above all, a teacher can communicate to you is what to read and *how* to read. How to read! For the art of reading is in danger of being lost among us. Reading is to be done with what Words-worth called "a wise passiveness". Youth must read so as to let the influence of a book really flow into the mind and heart. You cannot read with profit if you read combatively, disputatiously. First one must learn. Only later can one argue or dis-agree. You cannot truly read the great classics, ancient and modern, of the Jewish people with the dark and out-dated prejudices brought from your secularist High Schools; you cannot read these or, in truth, any other great classics with the equally out-dated nihilist views of the contemporary social scientist who, as a rule, brings nothing new to the information of forty years ago save the silly method of seeking to measure quantitatively the behavior of man and the monitions of man's spirit.

Yes, reading and right reading is core and center. Why should it not be? If you choose a major at college, you read, do you not? If you prepare your-self for the pursuit of a given calling, you read books, do you not? You read essential texts intensively; you seek, as best you can, to cover the field by extensive reading. In matters both sacred and pro-fane this is the method, since man has recorded all he has experienced and all he has learned through the medium of language, of the spoken, written, printed word. So, since you master all other subjects through books, it is evident that you must find your way back to Jewish knowledge and Jewish existence and Jewish integrity through books as well.

Strange that one has to say that! But recently in

America there arose very vocally a group of young Jewish scholars and writers who declared with apparent earnestness that they desired to be Jews once more. But they sought themselves out no teacher and allied themselves with no community of Israel and read all other books — the books of modern apostates and the books of anti-semites — but would read and study no Jewish books. That was and is neither very honest nor very intelligent.

There is, finally, a Jewish way of reading which Jews have cultivated for many centuries. In Yiddish and also in German it is called *lernen*. The fairly common Jewish patronymic Lerner is the name of him who in that specific sense *lernt*. What does this mean? It means a devout and *seeking* attention to the word of prophet or master; it means slaking a thirst of the soul. It means reading with the right and pure *kavanah*, intention, the right and pure aspiration after the sources of wisdom and of good. It desires to understand, not to argue; to absorb, not to brag with; to find words of life and follow them, not to find formulae for dispute or victory in dispute. It desires immersion into an eternal source of spiritual joy and rectitude. It seeks truth not triumph; it seeks God, not the world.

LAST WORD

After the great martyrdom and the small liberation in 1946, a little group of surviving Jews made their way Westward from Siberia whither the Soviet authorities had deported them. After many months of desperate hardships they reached the little Polish town that had been their home and their fathers'. The town was a mass of rubble. They did not find even graves. All their kith and kin had been burned alive in the crematoriums. The synagogue was in ruins. But a stair to a cellar had been saved. Descending that stair these Jews found a few Talmudic volumes, charred and water-soaked but still usable in part. And they procured them a few tallow-candles and sat down to read a page or two. There came one running then and cried: "Jews, do you forget that you are fleeing for your lives? The Soviets are closing the frontiers. The American zone is still far off! Flee!" And one of the group waved the messenger aside: "*Shah!*" he said gravely. "Be still. *M'darf lernen!* One must 'learn'."

We must all learn to "learn" once more.

Hints Toward Reading

HINTS TOWARD READING

I. FOUNDATIONS

The Holy Scriptures, Jewish Publication Society of America.

HERTZ, JOSEPH H., *The Authorized Daily Prayerbook*, Bloch.

COHEN, A., *Everyman's Talmud*, E. P. Dutton & Co.

GLATZER, N. N., *In Time And Eternity: A Jewish Reader*, Schocken.

II. INTERPRETATIONS

BAECK, LEO, *The Essence of Judaism*, Schocken.

BUBER, MARTIN, *Israel And The World*, Schocken.

GLATZER, N. N., *Franz Rosenzweig, His Life And Thought*, Jewish Publication Society of America.

HERBERG, WILL, *Judaism And Modern Man*, Jewish Publication Society of America.

HESCHEL, ABRAHAM, *The Earth Is The Lord's*, Henry Schuman.

LEWISOHN, LUDWIG, *The American Jew: Character And Destiny*, Farrar, Straus & Young.

III. CHRISTIAN INTERPRETERS

DUNCAN, J. GARROW, *New Light On Hebrew Origins*, Macmillan.

HERFORD, R. TRAVERS, *The Pharisees*, Bloch.

IV. ANTHOLOGIES

FLEG, EDMOND, *A Jewish Anthology*, Harcourt, Brace & Co.

KAPLAN, S. and RIBALOW, H. U., *The Great Jewish Books*, Horizon Press.

SCHWARTZ, L. W., *The Jewish Caravan*, Rinehart.

———, *A Golden Treasury Of Jewish Literature*, Rinehart.